Original title:
The Scarf's Silent Story

Copyright © 2025 Creative Arts Management OÜ
All rights reserved.

Author: Levi Montgomery
ISBN HARDBACK: 978-1-80586-172-0
ISBN PAPERBACK: 978-1-80586-644-2

Weaving Through Shadows of Yesterday

In a drawer where dust bunnies play,
Lies a fabric that's seen better days.
It danced with flair at a knitty soirée,
Now tangled in tales that continue to sway.

Once it snugged a neck with style so grand,
But now it's a hat for a very small hand.
Its colors a riot, flamboyant and bland,
A fashion faux pas—who wrote this demand?

It witnessed a sneeze that could move the world,
While warm hugs it gave, many twirls it unfurled.
A threadbare magician, with magic unfurled,
Its antics remind us of laughter swirled.

In the twilight, it whispers a chuckle or two,
As socks in a drawer spin wild tales anew.
And when you pull it out, what trouble it'll brew,
A woolly reminder of mischief in view!

Soft Hues of Memory's Embrace

In a pile, it lay with flair,
A knitted blob beyond compare.
With colors bright, yet quite askew,
It whispers tales of friends and brew.

Loomed by hands both wise and bold,
It tells of nights when warmth was sold.
A missing stitch, a tangled mess,
Yet still it wraps, a cozy dress.

The Chronicles of a Threadbare Love

Once so vibrant, now quite thin,
It quivers soft, a threadbare grin.
With every hug, it lets out sighs,
A love so grand, with frayed goodbyes.

Stitches seek a brand new fate,
Yet here it lies, not worth the rate.
In closets deep, it hides with pride,
An ancient love that won't subside.

Twisted Yarn of Winter's Breath

Amidst the chill and frosty air,
The yarn entwines in playful dare.
With every twist, a giggle springs,
As snug as bugs on winter's wings.

It weaves a tale of warmth and cheer,
Of snowball fights and hot cocoa near.
But watch it dance, it's quite a sight,
A rogue that twirls, escaping tight.

Cloak of Warmth, Veil of Stories

Cloaked in tales of days gone by,
It wraps the shoulders, oh so spry.
From first embrace to teary laugh,
It carries memories, a cozy gaffe.

Threads once bright now fade away,
Yet each mark tells of joy and play.
In winter's grip, it spins its yarn,
A silly tale, with charm to warn.

From Dusk Till Dawn: The Warmth Remains

A tangled twist, oh what a sight,
This messy yarn brings pure delight.
Wrapped around, I'm quite the clown,
With every turn, I fall right down.

In chilly air, I strut with pride,
Fuzzy threads, my warmest guide.
Laughing friends, we trade our tales,
Each stitch a giggle, all that prevails.

A Narrative of Past Embraces

Once I wore it to the fair,
Dancing with joy, without a care.
A gust of wind takes me for a spin,
Now it's a hat? Oh, where's my chin?

With coffee spills and buttery fries,
This trusty piece still never lies.
It tells of fun, of joy, of glee,
Each patch a story, just like me.

The Binding of Memory and Comfort

Stitch by stitch, I bind my heart,
Through every laugh, we're never far apart.
A puppet show of vibrant hues,
Quirky patterns, oh, what a muse!

Each time I trip, it hums a tune,
To every mishap, it'll swoon.
In moments silly, and blunders grand,
This funny tale forever will stand.

Souls Entwined in Yarn

Oh what fun, a friendly game,
Threaded chaos, never the same.
We laugh and spin, in loops and curls,
This tangled yarn brings out our whirls.

Along the road, in style we boast,
With every knot, we raise a toast.
For memories made with threads divine,
The laughter woven, forever will shine.

The Unspoken Language of Threads

In the drawer, a tangled mess,
Each thread whispers, 'I did my best.'
Colors clash, but oh, what fun,
A fabric dance, we're all but one.

The needle's laughter, oh so bold,
Stitches tell tales, both new and old.
A patchwork memory, sewn with glee,
Like a jester's cap, it's prancing free.

Fabric Paths of Time's Journey

Once a ribbon, bright and proud,
Lost in pockets, it screams out loud.
Persistent in whimsy, it threads the tale,
Through laughter, mishaps, offbeat trail.

Beneath the couch, it starts to plot,
A game of hide and seek—oh dear, forgot!
Jumps to the floor in a joyful roll,
Every twist and turn adds to its goal.

The Knitted Embrace of Years

With every row, a giggle's spun,
Woolly arms hug, warm as the sun.
A calendar of yarn, so brightly styled,
Each loop a memory from a playful child.

In winter's chill, they dance with care,
A crazy quilt fair, beyond compare.
Forgetful fingers make silly knots,
While mischief brews in cozy spots.

Colors That Hold Our Secrets Tight

Every hue hides a funny tale,
Like sock puppets that giggle and sail.
Quietly bold in a yarn basket's grip,
Whispers of laughter, on a colorful trip.

Stitched in shadows, they plot and scheme,
Chasing the cat, oh, what a dream!
With every tear, they start to laugh,
Secrets in stitches—our secret craft.

Wrapped in Tender Reminiscence

In the drawer, lies a twist,
A fabric holding memory's kiss.
Its colors fade, yet stories bloom,
A tangled tale in every room.

It once graced a neck, oh so proud,
Now it trips over shoes in a crowd.
It whispers jokes of colder days,
While in laundry, it always plays.

A cat once claimed it as a throne,
While I searched high and low, alone.
Who knew yarn could hold such fun?
An heirloom battle we've both won!

So here it sits, a playful mess,
Crafting joy in its soft caress.
A laugh or two, it brings each time,
Wrapping moments sweet as any rhyme.

Tales Inscribed in Soft Fibers

A bundle of threads with mischief brims,
Each fiber boasts of laughter's whims.
Knits and purls in colors bright,
Whispering secrets left and right.

Once it was worn at a grand ball,
Now it just welcomes the dust's sprawl.
It danced with glee, swirled in delight,
Now it's a cape for my funny pet site.

Hats of laughter and mittens of cheer,
Unraveling tales we hold so dear.
From chilly walks to cozy nights,
It's seen the fun in our silly fights.

Wrapped around dreams, it giggles low,
As I ponder where the lost socks go.
A patchwork of stories, bold and amusing,
In soft fibers, pure joy is fusing.

The Woven Heartstrings

Tangled threads tell stories anew,
Of wild adventures and morning dew.
Once a prince's cloak, now a laugh,
In rib-tickling tales, it's my other half.

Stolen from the floor by youthful paws,
It has seen heart, mischief, and applause.
Wrapped around my feisty face,
A playful wink in this cozy space.

It traveled the globe, or so it claims,
With tales of frogs and funny games.
Yet in the corner it sits to-day,
Reminding me of the fun we play.

A tapestry woven with giggles and grins,
With a twist and a knot where the laughter begins.
In every thread, a memory stuck,
Of joyful moments and enough good luck.

A Symphony of Tactile Memories

Once it twirled on a windy street,
Now it's soup-themed, quite a treat.
Soft threads tell of soup spills galore,
While I chase shadows across the floor.

It danced with grace, it jived with cheer,
Now entangled with socks that disappear.
Each fabric twist a humorous cue,
Reminders of joy like a peekaboo.

From chilly evenings by the fire,
To being a ghost in a schoolyard choir.
With every fold, it shares delight,
A symphony of giggles in moonlight.

A quirky partner in my play,
Bringing brightness to every day.
In threads soft as whispers, fables spin,
A tactile treasure where laughter begins.

The Warmth of Absent Embraces

A knot was tied, yet you slipped away,
My woolly hug, just a game we play.
Your laughter echoing, oh what a chat,
While I sit here, feeling quite flat.

Left on the hook, a joke in the air,
As I drape my warmth, you simply don't care.
In layers of yarn, I wrapped up my cheer,
But it unraveled when you disappeared.

Weaving Together Silent Goodbyes

Stitch by stitch, we said our farewells,
In patterns of loss, my loneliness swells.
A twist in the fibers, a playful retreat,
Yet here in my closet, your memories meet.

Each loop that I make brings a smile or frown,
A colorful yarn in our love's crazy town.
With every pull, I laugh and then sigh,
How did you manage to wear me so dry?

Echoes of Love in Every Loop

In every loop, a whisper of glee,
Played tag with joy, but you just let me be.
Your humor wove into my very seams,
Now I'm just tangled in confusing dreams.

From purls to knits, we danced through the years,
Knocking back pints, forgetting our fears.
Now I'm a relic, draped upon a hook,
A vintage tale, just read in a book.

Threads of Comfort and Reflection

Knitting my thoughts, I chuckle and grin,
Reflecting on moments, where to begin?
Your antics still swirl in my cozy wear,
While I count stitches, I can't help but stare.

A fabric of laughter, a sweater with style,
With every warm thought, I can't help but smile.
Though you're absent, your spirit is near,
I'll keep knitting on, oh, my dear, my dear.

Memories Wrapped Tight

In a closet, tightly coiled,
Colors twist, and patterns spoiled.
Each fold a laugh, a giggle or two,
Of parties gone by and a dance so skewed.

With polka dots and stripes galore,
It holds secrets of a blissful chore.
An unexpected wrap around the waist,
Turns a normal lunch into a wild haste.

Textures of a Life Lived

Silk slips through fingers with a whoosh,
While wool pulls back like a scared booosh!
Cotton whispers tales of summer's grace,
And blends old scenes in a cozy embrace.

A patchwork tale from the thrift shop's find,
Each seam a stitch in the fabric — kind.
Who needs a scrapbook when you have threads,
Spinning history's yarns while avoiding the spreads?

Chronicles Carried Close

Tucked in a bag, journey to fate,
A twisted knot seems to celebrate.
As I wear it on sunny days so bright,
It throws shade and giggles, oh what a sight!

From coffee spills to the snooze at noon,
It's a jester's cloak — a soft buffoon.
It slices through laughter, humor on cue,
This quirky companion, oh what it can do!

An Heirloom of Heartfelt Remnants

Passed down from grandma, a relic and tease,
It flapped in the breeze with a comic sneeze.
Swirled with the stories, a family delight,
Making everyone chuckle, from day into night.

Faded stains tell of feasts and spills,
Tales of mishaps and unexpected thrills.
It winks from the corner, a cheeky affair,
This heirloom wraps memories with flair!

Looming Shadows of Yesterday

Once a vibrant hue of bright red,
Hiding secrets in a cozy bed.
Now it sits with frayed edges, so cool,
A ragged piece of fabric, oh what a fool!

It witnessed a dog chase a cat,
Twisted around a lazy old hat.
Danced through the fun at a summer fair,
Now it snoozes without a single care.

When the kids played hide and seek around,
That fabric flew up and swirled around.
Tales of adventure draped on a chair,
Yet now it just clings to dusty air.

In a drawer it lies, with stains and cheer,
Documenting laughter of yesteryear.
Though it may be worn with a silly plot,
This fabric has stories that can't be forgot.

The Hidden Stories of Fabric

Underneath the folds, a tale does lie,
Of spilled grape juice and a slice of pie.
Each stain a giggle, every tear a laugh,
This fabric's tales deserve a paragraph!

It met a cat that thought it a toy,
Bungee jumping kittens brought so much joy.
With every tug, it wiggled in glee,
A funny old relic, like a giddy spree.

Once it dressed up a very brave lad,
He spun around, oh it looked so rad!
But then the wind grabbed it, what a flight,
Off it went, a comical sight!

Its colors may fade, but its spirit's bold,
In every crinkle, a memory told.
Though forgotten in a box, don't you see?
This fabric's adventures are wild and free!

Whispers of Worn Threads

With threads that whisper secrets of fun,
This old piece of fabric, bright like the sun.
It once housed a spill of raspberry jam,
Now it's just an amusingly sticky sham.

Alas, it's been through the wildest of nights,
Where it curled with laughter and playful fights.
A puppet show with socks and old shoes,
It's seen every trick and a comical ruse!

A game of dress-up, a crown for a doll,
It thought it was royal, standing so tall.
Yet now in the corner, it giggles in dreams,
Of adventures past, where silliness beams.

So next time you see it, don't toss it away,
For hidden within are the joys of the day.
Worn but not weary, it holds a spree,
This fabric's a treasure, wild and free!

Tapestry of Forgotten Journeys

Once a blanket for a tiny pet mouse,
Now it rests in an abandoned old house.
With quirks of colors, so daring and bright,
It hides the laughter of many a night.

In the closet it dreamed of picnic spreads,
While imaginary creatures danced on beds.
Up it flew to join the winds of play,
Catching all the chuckles along the way.

It draped over shoulders of actors in town,
In a farcical play, it earned a crown.
But with years it has mellowed, so charmingly old,
A patchwork of journeys, stories told.

So if you unravel its lovely seams,
You'll find silly stories stitched into dreams.
This tapestry holds a treasure so sweet,
A laugh in each thread, a whimsical feat!

Patterns of Past Heartbeats

In a drawer, it waits and sighs,
With mismatched patterns, oh, what a surprise!
It tells of dinners, spills, and jests,
Of happy hours and questionable vests.

Every thread a giggle, a tale undone,
Like who wore it last—was it grandma or son?
It dances in dreams with a quirky flair,
Spinning yarns of laughter floating in the air.

Threads of Fate Entwined

Twisted up with dust and a sock,
Once it kept warmth from sun till dock.
Dropped by a cat, snagged by a shoe,
Each tangle a laugh in this fabric zoo.

Around the necks of gnomes it glows,
Telling secrets only the brave one knows.
A ninja disguise, or a pirate's cap,
It dreams of adventures, of mishaps with a clap.

The Warmth of Unfurling Wings

Once it flew high on a rollercoaster ride,
Now it flops around on a dog's backside.
Fluttering here, wrestling with fate,
Chasing after cake crumbs—oh, how great!

It whispers of flights that never took off,
Of being a cape for a toddler's scoff.
Each twist a giggle, each fold a cheer,
On a wild adventure, in good fun, never fear!

Woven Memories on a Winter's Breath

Frosty mornings, tangled in glee,
A patchwork of stories as silly as can be.
It dreamt of snowflakes, of snowball fights,
But ended up lost in indoor delights.

Rewrapped on couches, bursting with cheer,
It snugged up the cat on a cozy veneer.
Each knot a giggle, a yarn of surprise,
Underneath laughter, where warm memory lies.

Silken Hues and Hidden Histories

Once owned by a parrot named Lou,
Who fancied himself quite the fashion guru.
He draped it with flair, oh what a sight,
As he strutted around, taking flight!

A slip on the floor made him spin,
Landing in a soup, oh where to begin?
The chef laughed so loud, quite the delight,
As Lou ruffled up, what a silly fright!

Now the scarf hangs high, on display,
With stories of birds who went out to play.
It sways with the breeze, a whimsical tale,
Of a parrot who thought he could sail!

Veils of Time Unraveled

In a drawer of oddments, hidden from view,
Lives a fabric that's seen quite the crew.
Once wrapped around a garden gnome,
Who claimed it was his very own home!

With buttons and bows, the gnome would boast,
Of parties at night with a ghostly host.
He'd tap dance and twirl in a faded light,
While the scarf just sighed, what a funny sight!

Now it whispers tales of mischief and cheer,
Of gnomes and ghosts who once danced here.
Each stitch holds laughter, both soft and sweet,
In a closet of memories, quite the treat!

A Tapestry of Unvoiced Emotions

Stitched with care but lost its glow,
A garment that felt quite the blow.
It's wrapped around a cat named Fuzz,
Who thinks it's a throne, what a buzz!

He struts and puffs, feeling so grand,
While humorous thoughts run through the land.
The neighbors chuckle at his royal air,
As Fuzz rules the home without a care!

But oh, what secrets could it reveal,
Of a feline who thinks he's the real deal.
Each fold holds laughter, each thread a jest,
In a life of comfort, he loves the best!

The Blanket of Untold Journeys

Once a wrap for a bumbling bear,
Who tumbled and rolled without a care.
He wandered through forests, near and far,
Claiming the world, like a bizarre star!

With honey on his paws, he'd have a feast,
While the scarf held tales of each honeyed beast.
It fluffed in the breeze, sang songs of delight,
Of a bear's escapades in the moonlight!

Now it lies snug, with stories to hold,
Of laughter and friendships, forever bold.
Each twist in its fiber, a giggle or two,
Of a bear and his scarf, always sweet and true!

Stitches of Remembrance

In the attic, it sits, full of flair,
Knitted by grandma with the utmost care.
Each loop a story, a giggle or two,
Twisting like tales of a mischief crew.

Lost at the party, oh what a sight,
Wrapped 'round a lamp, oh what a fright!
The dog wore it proudly, a very fine hat,
Chasing his tail, how funny is that!

Coffee stains mark the adventure of spice,
Spilled all the drama, oh isn't that nice?
Patterns of laughter, a threadbare design,
Every fiber a whisper, a punchline divine.

Hiding in shadows, where secrets reside,
Whispers of laughter, in stitches, they bide.
So here's to the yarn that binds us so tight,
With every mishap, we burst into light!

The Language of Layers

Wrapped round my neck, with colors so bold,
This sneaky old garment has stories untold.
A piece for each season, oh what a twist,
Donning my humor, it simply insists.

It once caught the ketchup, from a hot dog race,
Only to rescue a squirrel in a chase.
A fashionable armor against winter's dread,
With each layer added, my instincts misled.

Who knew it would catch the attention of cats?
Glistening brightly, a feast for the rats.
In a fashion parade, the pets take the lead,
This awkward ensemble, a hilarious breed.

But as I unwrap all these layers with glee,
The laughter erupts, it's not just for me.
In every small fold, there's a tale full of fun,
In the language of threads, we all come undone!

Shadows Wrapped in Warmth

Once I wore it on a chilly old day,
But it flew off my neck and ran far away!
Chased it down alleys, in the puddles it splashed,
Right into a bush, it devoured my cash.

In the sun, it danced with a playful breeze,
Creating such shadows, an artist's tease.
It tickled my nose as it sailed through the air,
Who knew it could dance? Oh, what a rare flair!

Then came the day, it tangled with dreams,
Wrapped around wishes, and muffled my screams.
In laughter, I found it, a comfort from knots,
A blanket of joy, tied with silly thoughts.

So here's to the shadows that wrap us with cheer,
In every odd twist, there's giggles to hear.
Under its cover, we find warmth and play,
Each knot a reminder—life's whimsical sway!

Memories in Every Fold

In every fold, there's a chuckle or two,
A slip from the laundry, that nobody knew.
Oh, the adventures this fabric has seen,
From fancy gala balls to sneaky cuisine.

Once mistaken for a picnic attack,
It joined the feast and wouldn't hold back.
Ham sandwiches stuffed in a pocket with flair,
What a wild moment, a soft, fragrant affair!

Wrapped tight around me for warmth and for jest,
It laughs in the corner, it knows I'm a mess.
A pair of old mittens, in hiding they play,
Crafting mistakes in the silliest way.

Memory-laden, with giggles galore,
In every soft wrinkle, it opens up doors.
So here's to the laughter that threads through our days,
With every fold's secret, we join in the play!

Frayed Edges of Remembrance

Threads unwind, tales untold,
Colors fade, but laughs are bold.
Knots of yarn, they twist and twine,
Each stitch a giggle, oh so fine.

A tangled mess, we wear with pride,
Fashion faux pas, we just can't hide.
With pom-poms bouncing, vibrant glee,
Worn like a crown, just wait and see!

Memories stitched with a dash of flair,
In every loop, a silly stare.
As seasons change, the colors clash,
But in our hearts, the joy won't dash.

A frayed edge here, a tear there too,
Each imperfection brings something new.
Around we go, in style's embrace,
A laugh, a hug, the perfect space.

Interwoven Dreams and Longing

Threads of laughter, dreams collide,
In a twisty yarn, our secrets hide.
Patterns shift, oh what a show,
Whirls of wishes, watch them flow.

A scarf of tales, each color a scream,
Knitted together, we share the dream.
The blues of hope, the reds of cheer,
With every loop, we conquer fear.

We wear our past, it snugly fits,
A cozy wrap of clever wits.
With every knot, a chuckle's born,
In the warmth of yarn, we're never worn.

So let the winds laugh, let them tease,
We'll dance with colors, move with ease.
In the tapestry of silly things,
Our hearts entwined, joy forever sings.

Textures of Tender Connection

Each fiber soft, a tale we weave,
In tangled threads, we learn to believe.
Every cuddle carries whispers sweet,
In the woolen warmth, our hearts repeat.

With frizzy ends and fuzzy charm,
Who knew a scarf could cause such alarm?
A twist, a tug, laughter rings out,
As we cozy up, there's never a doubt.

The patterns mush, a chaotic spree,
Yet in this chaos, we're ever free.
A swatch of hope, a dash of fun,
Wrapped in laughter, two become one.

Unraveled stories, shared with pride,
Every loop, a joyride.
In the cozy corners of this embrace,
A tapestry of giggles fills the space.

The Warmth Beneath A Sky of Grey

Under cloudy skies, we wrap up tight,
Colors twinkle, oh what a sight!
With every fold, a chuckle's near,
Embracing warmth, letting go of fear.

A scarf that dances in the breeze,
Fluffy fun that puts us at ease.
Each layer thick with warmth and cheer,
As storm clouds gather, we draw near.

Laughter loops, oh what a craze,
In the softest hug, we find our ways.
With every twist, a friendly tease,
In this whimsical world, we tease the freeze.

So when the winds howl, we'll laugh and play,
For with every thread, we light the way.
In a sky so grey, our colors rise,
Together we shine, with merry eyes.

Old Threads, New Stories

A tangled string in a drawer waits,
Whispers of laughter, ignored by fate.
Last winter's dance with a cat on the floor,
Map of mischief, memories galore.

Each knot a tale, each fray a giggle,
Once draped on shoulders, now curls and wiggle.
An old friend clings, through soda and snacks,
With every twist, it never quite slacks.

Hats that once puzzled, now stand on a shelf,
Jokes in the fibers, just like myself.
Threadbare emotions, they still hold sway,
In stitches and snickers, come what may.

So here's to the yarn that still brings delight,
Tales cozy and wild, from day into night.

Weaves of Time

Once wound so tightly, now looser it seems,
The patterns of life fray at the seams.
Brought out for warmth when the chill comes around,
Hilarity drapes, where giggles abound.

A colorful patchwork of blunders and wins,
Each pull on the thread makes old laughter spin.
All the foolish moments now wrap us with cheer,
Weave them together for smiles near and dear.

This fabric was worn at a dance, quite absurd,
With shoes that were squeaky, how could it be blurred?
But through each warm stitch, the fun never fades,
Time's colorful tapestries lend us parades.

Remember the day with spaghetti on heads?
Laughter's the thread that we tirelessly spread.
So mock the old yarn, but do not forget,
In laughter we weave, there's not a regret.

Touch of Memory

A faded old lump in the corner it sits,
Full of mishaps and joyful little bits.
Each loop a reminder of days that were bright,
And tangled-up tales that dance in the night.

Puppies and puddles, it soaked up with glee,
Adventures of kittens, climbing a tree.
Every loose thread roughens the fabric of time,
It's silly and warm, a comical rhyme.

With every unravel, there's memory's load,
Scraps from the laughter, commuters on road.
Wind them together, those stories now told,
In stitches of joy, our hearts become bold.

Draped on the couch, when the rain starts to pour,
It cradles our humor, an old friend we adore.
For warmth is not measured by patterns of style,
But in moments that spark joy, make us all smile.

The Embrace of Forgotten Warmth

In a box of oddments, an heirloom awakes,
With holes in its history, yet never forsakes.
It snickers in whispers of balmy delights,
Where stories were spun on the long winter nights.

Oh, the raucous escapades tucked in each fold,
From BBQ blunders to secrets retold.
A cozy companion through thick and through thin,
With threads of hilarity woven within.

It hugged me through winters, a soft, silly swipe,
Saw me dodge water balloons, how did I type?
Its fibers now fuzzy, it chuckles and beams,
Recalling old follies, bursting at seams.

So here's to the warmth, though frayed it may be,
Bringing back laughter, just sits there with glee.
With every embrace, it softens the heart,
In the humor of textiles, we never depart.

Stories Nestled in Twisted Yarn

Once bright and bold, now faded and frayed,
Hiding stories of laughter, a grand escapade.
Untangling issues, like childhood's fine art,
Each loop's a connection that warms up the heart.

Do you remember the day when it bounced down the lane?
Or the time it got lost in the poor puppy's gain?
Every snicker and smile woven deep in the threads,
Twisted in yarn, where our happiness spreads.

A hat on the head, to help hide the curls,
It's been through all ages, with giggles and swirls.
Through whispers, its fiber embraces the past,
A tapestry woven with joy that will last.

So here's to the strands that have bridged all the years,
Carrying echoes of laughter and cheers.
In each silly knot, let's revel and play,
With every mishap, we humorously stay.

Embrace of Fabric Memories

In the drawer, a twist of lace,
It whispers secrets in its place.
Once a gift from Auntie Sue,
Now it hides, who knows why, boo-hoo!

Stains of ketchup and old mayo,
This fabric's got quite the tale to show.
A picnic mishap, oh what a sight,
It's lost its charm, but not its bite!

Who knew a hem could hold such cheer?
A misfit scarf with stories dear.
It waved to cats and neighbors too,
Hello from the laundry, I love you!

So here's to all the yarns we spin,
The odd shapes and colors that make us grin.
Embrace those folds with laughter loud,
For each thread holds joy, a fabric crowd!

Unseen Threads of Time

A tangled mess in the corner tight,
What stories lie hidden in plain sight?
Once a staple, now a muse,
Worn in ways the crowd won't choose!

Twirled up in grandpa's old chair,
Did it dance with dust or just sit there?
It has been flung over many a game,
Pretending to be a trophy – oh, what a shame!

Fastened tight with a quirky clip,
Did it join in with the buttercup trip?
While hiking up the hill it's caught,
It waved at a squirrel, or so I thought!

With each fold, it giggles too,
A silent witness, oh what a view!
So next time you untangle your life,
Remember the fabric, free from strife!

Colors of a Hidden Life

Red as a lobster backed in glee,
Once a head-turner, now a debris.
Worn proudly at the beach, like a star,
Now stays home, dreaming of afar.

Polka dots rally with stripes in a dance,
Unruly patterns, oh what a chance!
They throw a party when no one sees,
Who knew fabric could have such joie de vie?

Yellow smirks where blues do pout,
A game of colors, roundabout!
Crumpled and creased, they still have flair,
Such vibrant tales of laughter to share!

In the closet, they scheme and plot,
Defining life's chaos, but hey, why not?
With each colorful memory they weave,
Life's fabric design is fun to believe!

Echoes in Every Fold

A crumple here, a fold over there,
This ponderous fabric's lost its air.
Once an icon of class and style,
Now it serves dust bunnies for a while!

What tales does it have of a festive night?
Did it witness disaster or pure delight?
It quivered in laughter, oh what a jest,
This fabric of memories, it knows best!

In a game of hide and seek, it folds,
Sharing moments, it feels so bold.
Too many stories tucked in its seams,
A canvas of life woven with dreams!

Don't throw it out, just give it a twirl,
For in every crease lies a secret whirl.
Echoes of giggles and spirits so free,
This funny fabric will always be!

Stitching Together Time's Echo

Once a little thread had dreams,
Of running with the seams of jeans.
It tangled up in laundry fights,
And laughed at all those socky nights.

A patchwork heart, it danced with glee,
In pockets deep, where treasures be.
Stitching tales of laughter's call,
With memories sewn in a tiny ball.

Time ticked by, it held its ground,
Through twisty trails, it's laughter found.
An old hem's wink, a comedic fate,
In every fold, there lies a date.

So here's to threads with tales to spin,
In every loop, we find the win.
A tapestry of giggles ripe,
In every knot, a playful type.

An Old Companion's Whisper

Once wrapped around a neck so warm,
It witnessed every silly charm.
From fashion fails to quick escapes,
It's seen all styles and silly shapes.

When cozy nights brought tales untold,
And chilly winds made friends feel bold.
It giggled softly with each tug,
When laughter warmed its knitted snug.

With coffee spills and crumbs galore,
It's found its place on every floor.
A trusty sidekick, soft and neat,
Through every moment, bittersweet.

So here's to whispers of the past,
A wardrobe friend that's built to last.
In every twist, a story spins,
A cozy life where love begins.

The Layers Beneath Our Touch

Beneath the layers, stories hide,
Of playful pranks and crafty pride.
In wrinkled folds of playful yarn,
Lies a secret laugh, a joyful warn.

The first layer tells of winters bold,
While the next one giggles fierce and old.
Every thread a laugh, every stitch a cry,
In colorful chaos, we wonder why.

A tickle here, a tug right there,
It wrestles dust bunnies with flair.
The wear and tear of all things dear,
Whispering jokes for all to hear.

So peel away with gentle hands,
And discover joy that never stands.
In every twist, a chuckle zooms,
Layers of laughter in cozy rooms.

Deep Hues of Heartfelt Narratives

In shades of red and stripes of blue,
A saga unfolds, warm and true.
With every thread a giggle flows,
In deep hues where humor grows.

This tale begins with a jumpy knit,
That found a home where warmth would sit.
Adventures spun with every round,
In colors bright, absurdity found.

The drapes have seen some wild display,
Like when the cat dared to ballet.
Through spills of tea and cookie crumbles,
The laughter echoes, it never stumbles.

So here's to colors, rich and bold,
In every stitch, a tale retold.
Through deep hues, we rise and sway,
Crafting joy in a funny way.

Tales Threaded in Time

Once wrapped in a hug with flair,
Danced with the winds without a care.
Lost once in a busy old drawer,
Now it's a legend, oh, what a lore!

Brought laughter to chilly winter nights,
Worn by a clown in rainbow sights.
It tickles your nose and brings out a grin,
Oh, how it wraps memories akin!

Warmth Worn with Grace

A cozy embrace with colors so bright,
Transforming a chill into pure delight.
It's seen a parade of funny old folks,
Who've strolled and tumbled like silly jokes.

With frays and twists, tales start to unfold,
Worn by a granddad, oh so bold!
Each thread a giggle, each knot a cheer,
This merry companion, we hold it dear.

A Journey in Knitted Reflections

It wandered the town, strutted around,
Getting into mischief it truly found.
Twisting and turning through laughter and tears,
A whimsical witness to whimsical years.

From picnics to parties, it made its mark,
Serving as a pillow for impromptu parks.
Draped over ice cream, it melts hearts,
Woven into the world, it plays many parts.

Stories Speckled with Dust

In an attic long forgotten, it lay,
Full of dust bunnies and tales of play.
A caper of cats, a game of the past,
Each thread a memory, too funny to last.

An oversized beret on a mischievous pup,
Or a pirate's peg leg, fitting right up!
Through stitches and laughs, it holds all the fun,
In a world of yarn, it's the number one!

Timeless Weaves of Nostalgia

In a box, they lay all curled tight,
A cozy jumble in colors so bright.
Each stitch is a tale from long ago,
Of fashion wars waged in glorious flow.

From flapper times to disco's mad spins,
How did this relic end up with my bins?
I found a sock, and oh — what a mess,
Fashion left me, I must confess!

Crochet dragons and knit-tangled dreams,
In this old quilt, odd laughter still gleams.
I wear it with pride, but oh, what a sight,
Who knew nostalgia could make me feel light?

A relic reclaims its own fashion fate,
Gigs of laughter, let's celebrate!
As I strut down the street, with confidence bold,
In a patchwork of memories, no shame to unfold.

Soft Silhouettes of Lost Love

A scarf once worn with a blush and a grin,
Now drapes like a yawn, where romance has been.
Whispers of warmth in laughter's soft thread,
But lost in the closet, it dwells with the dead.

Was it an ode to my heart's wild embrace?
Or did I just wear it to cover my face?
Each fray tells a story of when we would dance,
Now I'm just twirling with an empty romance.

Knots tied with hopes, unravelling fast,
My love life's a sweater that's faded and past.
In every loose end, I find humor and cheer,
Though love wore a scarf, it would just disappear.

Yet every lost thread has a giggle or two,
Of love's mismatched socks and misguided woo.
With a wink to the past, I reopen the drawer,
And wrap it around me, let love roam once more!

Chronicle of Threads and Heartstrings

A band of colors, so mismatched and bold,
Each thread pulls a laugh from stories retold.
From kitchen mishaps to wild nights out,
These tangled tales leave no room for doubt.

Grandma's old stash, with a wink and a grin,
What kind of fashion were we destined to win?
My skills a disaster, for sure nothing neat,
Those patterns of chaos just can't handle heat!

Yet wrapped in the laughter of stitching gone wrong,
Is a melody sweet, and a chorus of song.
Each woven reminder a tickle of glee,
In threads of a life that was lived wild and free.

So here's to the fabric of farcical fate,
To heartstrings we tug with a giggle, not hate.
For in every snafu, we find the good part,
Of love in the stitches, and joy in the heart!

Warmth in the Threadbare

A ragged old blanket, but oh, so cherished,
Each thread a remnant, yet never perished.
"I'll fix it tomorrow!" I swear every night,
Yet here it sits, full of whimsy and light.

In the corners, I find all the crumbs of past meals,
Memories layered in fabric reveals.
The holes tell a tale of my cat's playful spree,
Who knew string and fluff would be fashion key?

Worn threads so cozy, a blanket of cheer,
I stumble and trip, yet find laughter near.
Each tear holds a story, each patch a delight,
In the warmth of the threadbare, everything's right!

So here's to the frays and to every old spin,
To garments of joy, and the laughter within.
Let's weave a new feeling with threads of our dreams,
For in this warm chaos, true happiness gleams!

Threads of Whispered Tales

In a drawer, where dust bunnies play,
Lies a scarf that danced on laundry day.
It twirled and spun, oh what a sight,
Tangled in socks, a comical fright.

Its fibers twist like gossiping friends,
Sharing secrets that never quite ends.
A ticklish thread with a cheeky grin,
Once a wide swirl, now a knot within.

At parties, it claims to be highly grand,
But tied to a chair? Oh, isn't it planned!
Jokes and jests wrapped in wooly embrace,
It teases the cat—what a silly chase!

But when the night falls, it snuggles close,
Whispering tales, like the best of prose.
Threads of laughter stitched so tight,
A scarf with stories, always in sight.

Woven Secrets in Twilight

This ribbon of fabric has seen much joy,
From flapper's neck to toddler's toy.
A twist and a whip, oh such flair,
It once tried to fly, just caught in midair.

In twilight hours, it drapes on a chair,
Playing dress-up and pretending sans care.
It sings silly songs in colorful hues,
A fashion faux pas that still gets to cruise.

Ruffled and tussled, it's had its go,
With patterns that change like a game show.
It tries to assert it remains haute,
But is often used as a fancy dustcoat.

In laughter, it weaves its old, funny tale,
Through mishaps and miracles, it will prevail.
Woven in humor, with mischief it beams,
A piece of the past, stitching together dreams.

Fabric of Forgotten Dreams

In the attic, under cobwebs and dust,
A fabric lies whispering, as it must.
Once a bold blanket, now a ragged strip,
It dreams of chases on a wild and lively trip.

A coat for a dog, or a snack for a mouse,
It's part of the play in this tiny house.
Stretched out on chairs, it tells silly jokes,
With each little ripple, it giggles and pokes.

From sunny picnics to rainy old nights,
It's been in the mix of quirky delights.
Forgotten by many but loving its role,
In fabric of dreams, it plays heart and soul.

Now it's a patch in a scrapbook of glee,
With stories held tight like a mystery key.
Though frayed at the edges, it's vibrant and bright,
A merry accessory, it shines in twilight.

A Symphony of Silken Echoes

In a closet symphony of silken delight,
A scarf once prized struggles in flight.
It flares and folds with a cheeky intent,
Conducting a show that none ever sent.

A twirl in the wind, the dog starts to chase,
It wraps round the post—oh what a disgrace!
With notes of mischief and puns intertwined,
It jokes with the buttons, quite unconfined.

Echoing laughter from balcony heights,
It dreams up escapades under starry nights.
The world can't see it hanging so proud,
But secretly revels in a fabric-fest crowd.

Each vibrant color sings its own tune,
Dancing with shadows beneath the warm moon.
In this light-hearted concert, so sprightly, it shows,
A timeless reminder that laughter just flows.

The Chronicles of Comfort

In the closet, a tale unfolds,
A scarf with quirks, and laughter it holds.
It dances with warmth, and tickles your chin,
Bringing smiles to faces, where giggles begin.

With patterns so wild, it flares like a clown,
Bright colors that chase away any frown.
Wrapped 'round a neck, it gives quite a show,
A cozy comedian, don't you know?

It whispers of warmth in the blustering breeze,
Adventures of warmth, from winters with ease.
So snugly it hugs, like a friendly old friend,
In jest, it reminds us, warmth never ends.

Each twist tells a joke, every fold a jest,
In the realm of fashion, it's surely the best.
With laughter unfurling, it leaps with delight,
This scarf of comfort makes everything bright.

Colors that Speak

A flash of neon, a hint of gold,
This merry design, never grows old.
It shouts and it giggles in shades so bright,
In the world of scarves, it's the life of the night.

Flashing its shades like a rainbow parade,
With stories of joy and the mischief it laid.
When draped on the shoulders of those feeling blue,
It bursts into laughter, in every hue.

The blues tell of oceans, the reds scream of glee,
Each color a character, wild and free.
Wrapped snug in its fibers, life's worries unwind,
It's a joyful reminder that happiness finds.

In gatherings they gather, those hues full of cheer,
With friends all around, there's nothing to fear.
As day breaks to dusk, the colors unite,
In this spunky creation, life feels just right.

Echoes Beneath the Weave

Stitches of giggles, a whimsical tale,
This scarf sings songs, never goes pale.
Its patterns are whispers from years gone by,
Each twist has a secret, and oh, how they fly!

It held in its folds the warmth of the sun,
With tales of adventures, each stitch has fun.
Beneath woven fibers, the laughter runs deep,
In cozy embraces, its stories won't sleep.

Each thread tells a legend of frolic and play,
Of antics and blunders that brighten the day.
So let's raise a toast to this fabric of flair,
For echoing laughter is found everywhere!

When wrapped in its folds, the world feels less grim,
A comedy club, with each colorful whim.
We wear it with pride, this jovial lore,
In the tales of the weave, we 'yarn' for more!

Embrace of the Tangled Yarn

Oh, tangled and twisted, what humor you bring,
With loops that keep chuckling, it's fit for a king.
A playful embrace, it's a circus of thread,
Each loop is a giggle, a jest that's well bred.

In the highest of winds, it refuses to stay,
Dancing in the breeze, like it's here to play.
With knots like a jester, it reigns supreme,
Bringing joy to the chilly, a soft playful dream.

With strands intertwining, there's mischief galore,
It tickles the senses, we keep wanting more.
Wrapped close to the heart, let the fun never cease,
In its yarny embrace, we find laughter's peace.

For every missed knit and each wobble and sway,
Brings chuckles and smiles in the most charming way.
So here's to the yarns that tangle and tease,
In this great fabric realm, we find joy with ease!

Silent Stitches

In the drawer it lies, so shy and small,
A twist and a turn, it covers it all.
With threads that gossip, in colors so bright,
It whispers of secrets through day and night.

Each knot a memory, each loop a laugh,
Tangled in stories but not on a path.
A fashion faux pas? Who cares in the end,
With humor and warmth, a trusty old friend.

One flick of the wrist, it dances with flair,
But caught on a chair? Oh, fashion does dare!
Through trips and spills, it always returns,
With chuckles to share, and lessons it learns.

So here's to the tales of a fabric so neat,
A joyful companion that's soft and discreet.
In every grim wrinkle, a laugh waits to bloom,
This silent story weaves joy in the room.

Loud Hearts

Bold colors shout from this bundle so tight,
A cacophony woven with threads of delight.
Each stitch a heartbeat, each fold a cheer,
Together they huddle, bringing good cheer.

An old lady sneezes, her treasure flies high,
Caught on a branch, oh how it does sigh!
It flaps in the breeze, like a comedic dance,
Making passersby grin, as if in a trance.

At the market it sold, the price made them frown,
Yet it's worth every penny, a steal in this town.
With laughter it stretches, making hearts swell,
A fabric of joy, with stories to tell.

So bring on the jests, let the giggles ignite,
For in laughter and warmth, life feels so right.
This loud heart of fabric, it sings every day,
As we wrap up in smiles and drift happily away.

The Fabric of Untold Tales

Once upon a time, in a closet it lay,
A patchwork of giggles stuck in dismay.
With polka dots dreaming of marbles and spins,
A tapestry woven with chuckles begins.

Grandma's old shawl with its ruffles and lace,
Hides tales of mischief and oh! what a race.
From tea spills to yarn fights, the stories unfold,
As laughter and warmth are lovingly told.

A cat with a penchant for climbing to peaks,
Found comfort in fabric, while chaos it seeks.
And the day that it snagged, pure pandemonium,
Left stitches of joy in our cozy coliseum.

So here's to the fabric with quirks in each seam,
A blanket of laughter, a whimsical dream.
For every soft whisper, there's humor to share,
In the fabric of life, we unravel with care.

A Journey in Every Weave

This fluffy old scarf, with its colors so wild,
Takes us on journeys, like a curious child.
From snowy escapes to a beach full of sun,
With every bright stitch, the fun's just begun.

A bobble on one end like a clown's big nose,
Sways with each step, as it giggles and glows.
Tangled in laughter, and oh! what a tease,
It plays hide and seek with the cool morning breeze.

Through ups and downs, it's along for the ride,
Like a trusty old friend who won't let you hide.
It whispers of adventures, both silly and sweet,
With every new weave, it dusts off your feet.

So here's to the journeys, with threads full of cheer,
This scarf knows the stories, let's lend it an ear.
As it dances with grace through each twist and each turn,
In the laughter of life, it's the joy we all yearn.

Secrets Woven in Warmth

A colorful weave, with secrets to share,
Like a jigsaw of stories wrapped up with care.
In each little fiber, a giggle resides,
A tapestry buzzing with joy that it hides.

The baby's first steps, the dog's wobbly race,
Caught in the pattern, oh the smile on its face!
From winter's cold chill, to a summer's warm glow,
This fabric holds laughter wherever we go.

With each little snag, it winks and it snorts,
Daring us into a world full of sorts.
Caught in a tree? It chuckles and weaves,
Wrapping us tightly in comfort it leaves.

So here's to the warmth, the laughter, the fun,
This quirky old fabric, our joy has begun.
With secrets encircled, it laughs and it stays,
Woven in kindness through all of our days.

Fragments of Memory

Once snug around a neck, so tight,
Now a blanket for a cat at night.
It's been through laughter, joy, and tears,
And still drapes on my own two fears.

Each fray tells tales of BBQ mishaps,
And busy days with hasty straps.
It once muted a sneeze mid-laugh,
Now it's just fabric, like a photograph.

Soft and Strong

Fuzzy thoughts on chilly days,
Like wearing your dog in various ways.
It cuddles close, yet makes a fuss,
What memories hold, we all discuss.

A fortress built for hugs and warmth,
But on dance floors, it exposes its charm.
A cape for snowball fights untold,
Space cowboy dreams in threads of gold.

Tales of Comfort Worn Thin

Oh, the stretch from the many wraps,
A faithful friend through nap-time naps.
But just like cheese, it's starting to smell,
With tales that only my dryer can tell.

Through spills and thrills, it clings so tight,
Yet in the wash, it gives me a fright.
I still hold it close, though the colors fade,
With patterns from parties that we've mislaid.

Weaving Whispers in the Cold

In winter's chill, it wraps me well,
But tells my secrets more than I'd tell.
Like a gossiping friend that's been around,
With every twist, a tale is found.

In the close of the night, it snickers loud,
Of shivering dances lost in a crowd.
It snags on the doorknob in a rush,
Resulting in an unplanned, silly hush.

Warmth Encapsulated in Fabric

Colors splashed like laughter bright,
Stitched with mischief, oh what a sight!
It warms my heart but steals my glances,
As it flirts with fashion in silly dances.

Yet every loop tells a funny reason,
For its existence through every season.
A jester wrapped around my spine,
A comic relief with every line.

The Quiet Language of Fabric

In a drawer the fabric lays,
Whispers of colors in splendid displays.
Tickling the air with their urge to sing,
Each thread a giggle, a funny little thing.

Fabrics of fortune, crinkle and grin,
Tales of lost socks and mischief within.
Quietly bundled, they plot and they scheme,
Who knew that a hem could laugh in a dream?

Quilts with the weight of stories untold,
Adding punchlines as the night turns cold.
Giddy as children, they sway with the breeze,
Each pattern a punchline that aims to please.

So next time you find some cloth in a heap,
Remember their giggles as you drift off to sleep.
For fabric can chatter, when left all alone,
In stitches and seams, a world of their own.

Threads that Bind the Past

Once a bright scarf on a whimsical flight,
Now tangled with tales of a comical night.
Snagged on a doorknob, it sways with a grin,
Recalling the moments of mischief and spin.

Grandma once wore it to the market so fair,
Povera made wagers on its colorful flair.
But a bump in the road, oh the yarns it could tell,
As a chicken ran past, it fell under a spell.

It spun through the air, a wild, flapping bird,
Tales of embarrassing falls with each playful word.
A connection of fabric, of laughter and tears,
Bound by the magic of whimsical years.

So when you unwind the threads of the past,
Remember the laughter, the fun that would last.
For beneath all the stitches, a warm, jolly fuss,
Intertwined with joy, in each snip and each thrust.

Echoes from a Cozy Haven

In a corner of living, where warmth seems to hum,
A blanket is chuckling, 'Here, pass me the crumb!'
With patches of stories, it holds in its fold,
Tales of a cat who thinks he's so bold.

The chair looks quite chummy, it's wobbling with glee,
As cushions converse on who'll spill their tea.
Rug's giggling softly, tickling the toes,
Bringing the dance of a snazzy foot pose.

A footstool's in stitches, a pun to unfold,
As visitors arrive, it's all chaos controlled.
And laughter erupts, echoing off the walls,
As fabric confesses, 'We had quite the ball!'

So come take a seat, share your tales of delight,
In this cozy haven, where echoes are bright.
Join in the laughter, let troubles be few,
In the warm weight of fabric, there's magic for you.

Patches of Unspoken Love

Stitched with a smile, these pieces unite,
A quilt of affection, snugly and bright.
Each patch tells a tale, with humor it weaves,
Of making sweet mischief while hiding your leaves.

A polka-dot corner, where laughter once sparked,
With jelly stains telling of moments quite stark.
Love's fleeting stitches, an inside joke shared,
Whimsical moments that no one declared.

Patches of joy, each dovetail so neat,
Where hearts meet with mischief, no chance to retreat.
Silly little secrets, tucked in each seam,
A fabric of memories, sewn in a dream.

So gather 'round closely, with chuckles in tow,
These funny, warm patches have stories to show.
And in every hemmed border, a giggle, a sigh,
The silent affection that never says goodbye.

Layers of Life and Legacy

In a drawer of wonders, it quietly lays,
Worn in odd places, on silly days.
A splash of beige, and a dash of green,
Each twist and turn holds a secret unseen.

Pulled out at parties, to humor the crowd,
Makes even the shy ones feel daring and loud.
Tangled in stories of laughter and glee,
Oh, what a life for a fabric to see!

A scarf like a time-machine, weaving through,
With every hug, it connects me and you.
Silly selfies, a wrap that won't quit,
It's a hero of antics - who knew it could fit?

So many layers, a legacy bright,
It's just a scarf, but it feels so right!
When life gets dull, give it a twirl,
A fabric of fun, in this vast, crazy world.

Threading Through Time's Embrace

A twisted tale in every fold,
With colors and laughter, it's pure gold.
Who knows where it's been, or whom it has met,
In every corner of joy and regret.

From grandma's attic to barista's hand,
Each thread a whisper, in life's grand stand.
Ah, the stories it shares as it swings,
Making mundane moments feel like kings.

A loop, a knot, a dance of delight,
It tickles the air, what a ridiculous sight!
In its warm embrace, the world takes a spin,
Threading through laughter, let the good times begin!

Sometimes a blanket, sometimes a show,
A legacy woven, just let it flow.
Through every mishap, it's always there,
A fashion faux pas? Oh, who would dare?

The Weaving of Solitude

Alone with a scarf, I twist and I twirl,
Making a fashion statement that's quite the whirl.
To the untrained eye, just a piece of cloth,
But I'm the model, and what a froth!

In solitude's grasp, it becomes a friend,
Wrapping me up till the awkwardness ends.
Oh, look at me, with my fabulous flair,
Daring to dazzle in the evening air!

I wave from my window, it dances in time,
The passerby giggles, they think it's a rhyme.
Turns out my scarf's got quite the charm,
Who knew wrapped in fabric, I'd raise the alarm?

Each thread's a giggle, each knot a joke,
Embracing the solitude, it's not just smoke.
In this quiet drama, I'm center stage,
A scarf-prince in a world that's all the rage!

Ghosts of Colors Past

Whispers of hues in a tangled embrace,
From days gone by, they scream with grace.
A riot of colors, a fashion parade,
Oh, look at that green! It was once a shade.

Each swirl and curl tells a story absurd,
Of moments that crashed, and laughter unheard.
The blue was a birthday, twinkling so bright,
Now it just laughs in a ghostly light.

In the shadow of memories, watch it unfold,
A carnival of threads, both timid and bold.
Faded pastels still light up the room,
A fabric of spirit, banishing gloom.

So here's to the colors that time can't erase,
A hauntingly funny, yet cheery embrace.
With each goofy thread, it giggles with glee,
A scarf of the ages, forever carefree!

The Fabric of Loving Farewells

Worn with love, it flaps in glee,
A cloth that begs, 'Don't forget me!'
Each swish and sway, a tale it tells,
Of all the hugs and cozy smells.

Draped around, it dances about,
Like a puppy ready to shout.
It whispers secrets, oh so sly,
While on the breeze, it flutters high.

In laughter's echo, it finds its place,
Tickled by wind, in a joyful race.
Off to adventures, it sways and spins,
In all its glory, the fun begins!

Each fold a giggle, a memory bright,
In a fabric world, pure delight!

Unfolding Stories in Every Fold

Under bright daylight, it unfolds wide,
With quirky patterns, it takes pride.
Each crease a wrinkle, a funny face,
Daring you to embrace its grace.

Worn when it rains, or shining sun,
It claims the title of everyone's fun.
With a flick and a twist, it plays along,
In the fabric dance, you can't go wrong!

Caught in the wash, with socks in a whirl,
It giggles out loud, as it starts to twirl.
Nothing phases its cheerful flair,
It winks at laundry, and jumps with air!

For every mishap, a chuckle behind,
In stories of fabric, joy you'll find.

Tides of Memory in Every Twill

With waves of color and tales to tell,
This twill has wandered, casting its spell.
From silly days under golden rays,
To stormy nights in a cozy blaze.

It tumbles around, with friends in tow,
Clinging tightly, as breezes blow.
From silly spills to dances at night,
This twill holds secrets, each one a bite!

The dryer spins laughter, the fabric gleams,
In the tides of joy, forever it dreams.
Mapping the moments, both big and small,
This playful cloth just loves to enthrall!

With each gentle rustle, it shares its lore,
Witty memories all set to explore.

Fabricated Memories from a Cold Night

Under starry skies, a blanket of cheer,
A fabric whispers, 'Come cuddle near!'
Each thread spins tales of warmth and glow,
In the frosty night, it steals the show.

Like a warm hug from a dear friend's heart,
It brightens the cold, playing its part.
In giggles and snuggles, a jolly sight,
This fabric's a laugh, oh what a night!

With marshmallow dreams and cocoa in hand,
It creates a magic, perfectly planned.
As stories unfold, wrapped snug and tight,
Embraces that linger until morning light.

When winter calls, it answers with glee,
Reminding us all, fun's the key!

www.ingramcontent.com/pod-product-compliance
Lightning Source LLC
Chambersburg PA
CBHW070005300426
43661CB00141B/248